W9-AFF-776

I·N·S·I·D·E
CHINA

Ian James

Franklin Watts
London · New York · Sydney · Toronto

CONTENTS

© 1989 Franklin Watts
96 Leonard Street
London EC2

Published in the USA by
Franklin Watts Inc.
387 Park Avenue South
New York, N.Y. 10016

Franklin Watts Australia
14 Mars Road
Lane Cove
NSW 2066

Design: K & Co
Illustrations: Hayward Art Group

UK ISBN: 0 86313 838 1
US ISBN: 0-531-10833-3
Library of Congress Catalog
Card Number: 89-8928

Phototypeset by Lineage Ltd, Watford
Printed in Belgium

Photographs: Chapel Studios 11t,
11b, 18t, 25, 27; Chris Fairclough 5t,
5b, 6, 7, 8, 9t, 9b, 10, 12, 13, 16t, 16b,
17, 18b, 19, 20, 21, 22, 23, 29, 30;
Hutchison Library 4, 15, 24t, 24b; S
Keeler 28.

Front cover: Chris Fairclough
Back cover: Chris Fairclough
Frontispiece: Chris Fairclough

The land

China is the world's largest country after the Soviet Union and Canada, but it has a larger population than any other country. More than one out of every five of the world's total population is a citizen of China.

Much of China is thinly populated. Most people live in the fertile river valleys in the east, especially in the lower valleys of the Huang He (or Yellow River), the Chang Jiang (or Yangtze), and the Xi Jiang (or West River) The southeast has a wet warm climate. Because of the weather, three or even four crops can be grown every year in some areas. East-central China is another rich farming region. The northeastern plains have hot summers, but winters are very cold.

Below: **Most of China's farmland is in the east. The northeastern lowlands have hot summers, though winters are extremely cold.**

Above: **The Huang He (or Yellow River) passes through the city of Lanzhou.**

Left: **The southern uplands in southeast China contain much scenic hill country.**

Only five per cent of the people live in the western half of China. In the southwest is the bleak, windswept Tibetan plateau. which is bordered in the south by the world's highest range, the Himalayas. This range includes Mount Everest, China's and the world's highest peak.

North of Tibet are deserts, including the Taklimakan, and rugged mountain ranges. The Gobi desert in north-central China has burning hot summers and bitterly cold winters. Between this desert and the eastern lowlands are the Mongolian border uplands. The yellow soil, called loess, of these uplands gives the Yellow River its name.

Above: **Mountains rise above a flat valley in the Tibetan Highlands in southwest China.**

The people and their history

China's history goes back about 4,000 years. Its early civilizations were marked by great achievements, such as the building of the Great Wall, which was more than 6,000 km (3,730 miles) long. China led the world in producing many inventions, including the compass, gunpowder, paper and porcelain.

The Chinese call themselves Han, after the Han dynasty which ruled China from 206 BC to AD 228. About 94 per cent of the Chinese are Han. They have a common written language, though hundreds of dialects are spoken. The other people in China belong to more than 50 minority groups, each with its own language and culture. Large minority groups include the Kazakhs, Koreans, Miaos, Mongolians, Tibetans, Uighurs, Yis and Zhuangs.

Below: **The Great Wall of China, the longest structure ever built, is the only artificial feature on Earth that can be seen by astronauts in space.**

China's last emperor was deposed in 1911. After civil war and a Japanese invasion in the 1930s, the Communist Party, led by Mao Zedong, won power in 1949. They began to turn China, a poor farming country, into a powerful industrial nation. They raised food production and set up new industries. Their methods were often cruel and many people were killed or put in prison. After Mao's death in 1976, the new Communist leaders removed laws preventing workers from earning extra money for themselves.

Above: **Terracotta (clay) statues of soldiers and horses were found in 1974 near Xi'an in the huge tomb of Qin Shi Huangdi, who became emperor in 221 BC.**

Left: **Statues and pictures of Mao Zedong, the country's Communist leader from 1949 to 1976, are common sights in China.**

Below: **Hong Kong is a small British colony on the southeast coast of China. Britain has agreed to return Hong Kong to China in 1997.**

Towns and cities

About 78 per cent of the people in China live in country areas. Some people, including some Kazakhs and Mongolians, lead wandering lives, herding livestock. These nomads live in tents, but most people live in large farming villages, in houses built from clay bricks or stone.

The largest city, Shanghai, stands on the delta of the Chang Jiang (Yangtze) river. The city grew quickly in the 19th century, when foreign merchants and diplomats lived there. Their homes and offices have given Shanghai a Western appearance. Shanghai is a major manufacturing city, producing about 10 per cent of China's industrial output.

Below: **This village is in east-central China. Most village homes have no electricity or running water.**

Right: **Guangzhou stands on the Zhu Jiang (Pearl River). Many people once lived in boats on the river. The government has moved most of these people into apartment buildings.**

Below: **Shanghai, on the Huangpu River, is a busy city with many Western-style buildings.**

Other major cities in China include Tianjin, southeast of the capital Beijing. It is a great trading and manufacturing city. Shenyang, the largest city in the northeast, and Wuhan, on the Chang Jiang river in east-central China, are other industrial cities. The largest city in the southeast is Guangzhou, which is also known as Canton. Guangzhou is a focus of international trade.

China has many attractive, historic cities. Xi'an is an old capital of China. It has many historic relics, including the famous terra-cotta army of 7,000 soldiers which was found there. Some cities, such as Lhasa, capital of Tibet (now the Xizang Autonomous Region) are very remote. Lhasa contains many Buddhist temples.

Above: **Lhasa is the capital of Tibet. On a hilltop stands Potala Palace, former home of the religious leader, the Dalai Lama. He fled to India, in 1959 after a Tibetan rebellion against the Chinese was defeated.**

12

Family life

Living standards have risen greatly since the Communist Party came to power in 1949. Food production has increased and new industries set up to make goods such as sewing machines and televisions which make family life more comfortable.

City people generally have higher living standards than country people. Many city people live in small apartments, which are owned by work units. Everyone belongs to a work unit, which may be a factory, a farm community, or some other group. Although wages are low, both parents usually work and grandparents care for the children during the day. Families were once large. But the government has limited the size of families by encouraging people to marry later and only have one child.

Below: **Many homes in country areas, such as these in Yunnan province in southern China, have no electricity or piped water supplies.**

Left: **Some city people live in small houses in the older districts, as here in Shanghai. Others live in apartments.**

Right: **Many country homes contain only essential items of furniture.**

16

Food

Major foods include wheat in the north and rice in the south. Vegetables, pork and poultry, are also important.

Beijing cooking, in the northeast, includes wheat noodles, stews, barbecues, and seafood. Crispy Beijing (or Peking) duck is famous. Huaiyang cuisine of east-central China includes steamed dishes, and in Shanghai, a great variety of seafood dishes. Cantonese cooking in the southeast is based on rice, with stuffed vegetables, shellfish and fish, including sharkfin soup. Inland, Sichuan cuisine is very spicey.

Below: **An open-air vegetable market in Wuxi, near Shanghai.**

Above: **An Uighur family in Kashi, a town in southern Xinjiang province in the far west of China.**

Left: **Chopsticks and spoons are the only utensils used to eat food. Tea is the most popular drink.**

Sports and pastimes

Physical exercise is an important part of Chinese life. Many people take part in early morning exercises in city streets. The young enjoy energetic martial arts, others prefer a graceful form of exercise called t'ai chi ch'uan. T'ai chi ch'uan developed from a 17th-century martial art.

The leading sports are those that do not require costly equipment. For example, concrete table tennis tables are common sights in parks or in the recreation areas of work units. In recent years, the Chinese have won much acclaim for their achievements in such sports as diving, table tennis and women's volleyball. Other popular sports include badminton, baseball, basketball, soccer and swimming.

Below: **The Chinese are internationally famous for their skill at table tennis.**

Many people work 50 to 60 hours a week. Men and women usually share domestic jobs such as cooking and cleaning. As a result, many Chinese have little time for leisure pursuits. However, most villages have a recreation area, with a small library and a television set. Some have choirs, orchestras and drama groups.

The cities have far more facilities, including museums, sporting and theatrical events and many classes and meetings. Photography is a popular hobby. Home activities include listening to the radio, watching television, making clothes and playing cards, though gambling for money is illegal.

Above: **Many older people perform ancient exercises, called t'ai chi ch'uan, every morning. These graceful exercises emphasize balance and good breathing.**

The arts

Early Chinese arts included pottery and jade carving. Buddhism, which was introduced into China during the Han dynasty (202 BC-AD 220), inspired sculptors to produce fine statues of the Buddha. Chinese literature, which goes back nearly 3,000 years, is some of the world's oldest. The earliest works were poems. Early prose works were concerned with Confucianism and Taoism, two forms of Chinese religion. Drama developed in the 13th century.

Calligraphy, the art of handwriting, began about 2,000 years ago. Working with brushes or with pens and ink, the artists often added calligraphy to paintings. For example, a painting of blossom on trees might include a poem about spring.

Below: **Calligraphy, or beautiful handwriting, is an art form in China. Calligraphy may appear on its own or it may accompany paintings.**

Chinese music uses a different scale from Western music, but Western symphonic music is also performed. Beijing opera is a form of drama based on ancient stories. It combines dialogue, songs and dance.

Mao Zedong believed that all art should have a political meaning, and serve the aims of the Communist Party. From 1966, China went through a period called the Cultural Revolution, which aimed to make China a completely classless society. Many artists were arrested and their works were destroyed or banned. Since Mao's death in 1976, books, dramas and other arts banned during the Cultural Revolution have again been made available to the people.

Below: **Dancers perform at a Full Moon Festival in Tibet.**

Farming

In the 1950s, Chinese farmers were organized in communes, which owned land and sold its produce to the government. Today, families farm the land. They give part of their crop to the commune and sell some to the government. But they keep the profits on the rest which formerly went to the commune. This has increased production. Only 11 per cent of the land is used for crops, and 31 per cent for grazing. Farming employs 74 per cent of China's workers. The main farming area is the southeast, where farmers grow rice, citrus fruits, peanuts, sugar cane, sweet potatoes and tea. In the northeast, wheat, corn (maize), millet and sorghum are grown.

Below: **Terraces for growing rice are built on many hillsides in southern China.**

Left: **Tea is grown in southeastern China. It is China's most popular drink.**

Below: **Pigs are the most important farm animals.**

Industry

China has huge natural resources. It is the world's leading producer of coal and it is among the top ten producers of iron ore, lead, manganese, tin, oil, uranium, gold, phosphates, salt and tungsten.

After the Communists took over in 1949, they were determined to make China a great industrial power. At first, they concentrated on heavy industry, such as steel, chemicals, machinery, ships, tools and commercial vehicles. Since the mid-1970s, many consumer industries have been set up to manufacture goods for the home. Today, China is the world's third largest producer of televisions. Other new industries are making such things as bicycles, radios, tape recorders, washing machines and electronic watches. China is also the world's leading producer of cotton fabric.

Below: **Workers in a commune factory in Xi'an make plastic shopping bags.**

	Industry		Tobacco
	Coal mining		Fruit
	Oil and gas fields		Silk
	Hydro electric station		Fishing port
	Sheep and goats		Wheat
	Camels		Rice
	Yaks		Cotton
	Pigs		Tea

The map shows some economic activities in China.

The northeast, especially around Shenyang, Beijing and Tianjin, has many industries. Other industrial regions include Shanghai and the cities around it, and Guangzhou in the southeast. Some industrial cities, such as Wuhan, Chengdu and Chongqing, lie inland.

Trade has expanded greatly in recent years. China imports machinery, iron and steel, chemicals and vehicles. It exports oil, food, textiles and clothing. China's leading trading partner is Japan. To speed up its industrial growth, China has set up five Special Economic Zones, five "open zones", and 14 "open cities". In these areas, China gives special advantages to foreign companies introducing new technology.

Below: **A silk spinning factory in the industrial city of Wuxi, near Shanghai.**

Looking to the future

China is now an important world power, but it remains a poor country. In 1987, its per capita Gross National Product (the value of all the goods and services divided by the population) was only US $300, as compared with $10,430 in Britain and $18,430 in the United States.

China plans to become a "middle developed" country by the year 2050. It has introduced many economic reforms. These permit people to make profits and foreign companies to invest in China and to modernize its industries. The Chinese government is also trying to control the growth of the population and eventually, reduce it. But its policy of limiting the size of families has proved very unpopular.

Below: **Posters are used to encourage parents to have only one child.**

China faces other problems. The benefits of the reforms are not equally shared. Parts of the southeast have become prosperous, but life in the north and west is still hard. Many workers have found that the benefits of extra income are wiped out by rising prices.

China is changing economically, but political change is slow. China is still a Communist country and the liberty of the people is restricted in many ways. In 1989, many students in the cities held huge demonstrations, asking for more democracy. The government crushed their hopes in a bloody massacre and later executed many protestors.

Above: **Education is regarded as an essential part of China's plans to develop its economy and raise living standards.**

Facts about China

Area:
9,560,000 sq km
(3,691,463 sq miles)

Population:
1,064,147,000 (1987)

Capital:
Beijing

Largest cities:
Shanghai (pop of city,
    suburbs 12,050,000)
Beijing (9,470,000)
Tianjin (7,990,000)
Shenyang (4,200,000)
Wuhan (3,400,000)
Guangzhou (3,290,000)
Chongqing (2,780,000)

Official language:
Chinese

Religions:
Buddhism, Taoism,
Christianity, Islam

Main exports:
Oil and oil products,
food, textiles and
clothing, chemicals

Unit of currrency:
Renminbi or Yuan

China compared with other countries

China 108 per sq.km.

Britain 231 per sq.km.

USA 26 per sq.km.

Australia 2 per sq.km.

Above: **China is less densely populated than Britain.**

Below: **China is larger than the United States.**

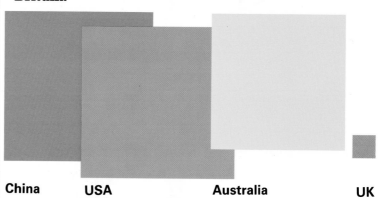

China   USA   Australia   UK

Below: **Some Chinese stamps and money.**

UNION OF SOVIET SOCIALIST REPUBLICS

MONGOLIA

Dahinggan Mountains

• Harbin

• Changchun

Tien Shan Mountains

Shenyang •

• Yining   • Urumqi

Hohhot

Gobi Desert

Anshan

N. KOREA

(Yellow River)

Beijing

Dalian

R. Huang He

Yinchuan

Tianjin

Bo Hai Gulf

S. KOREA

Taklimakan (Desert)

Qilian Shan

Taiyuan

• Yumen

Lanzhou

Shijiazhuang

Jinan

Kunlun Shan

Zhengzhou

Qingdao

• Xining

Xi'an •

Huang Hai
(Yellow Sea)

Wuxi

Nanjing

Shanghai

Tanggula Range

Chengdu

R. Chang Jian
(Yangzi)

Wuhan

Suzhou

Kizang (Tibet)

Hangzhou

Mount Qomolangma

R. Yarlung Zangbo

Chongqing

Nanchang

NEPAL

(Mt Everest)

Lhasa

Changsha

BHUTAN

Dong Hai
(East China Sea)

BANGLADESH

R. Nujiang

Guiyang

Guilin

INDIA

Lancang Range

Kunming

Nan Ling Mountains

Fuzhou

Taiwan

BURMA

Wuzhou

Guangzhou

Hong Kong (UK)

Nanning

Macao (Portugal)

LAOS

Hainan

THAILAND

Nan Hai (South China Sea)

PHILIPPINES

CAMBODIA
(Kampuchea)

VIETNAM

SRI LANKA

MALAYSIA

INDONESIA

0   200   400 miles

0   200   400   600 km

Index